This book belongs to:

_____

A catalogue record for this book is available from the British Library

Published by Ladybird Books Ltd
80 Strand London WC2R ORL
A Penguin Company

2 4 6 8 10 9 7 5 3 1
© LADYBIRD BOOKS LTD MMVIII
LADYBIRD and the device of a Ladybird are trademarks of Ladybird Books Ltd

ISBN: 978-1-84646-937-4

Printed in China

My best book about...

Diggers

Written by Mandy Ross
Illustrated by Liz and Kate Pope

What a lot of diggers and dumpers!
Which one would you like to drive?

Here's a busy building site.

What job is each digger doing?

Can you help the dumper driver find the way to deliver his load of gravel?

Gravel

Welcome to the digger factory!

How many red diggers are there?

Here are some other things that builders use.

Can you find them all in the picture?

These diggers are helping to build some houses.

Have you ever seen a house being built?

These diggers have delivered some bricks, sand and gravel.

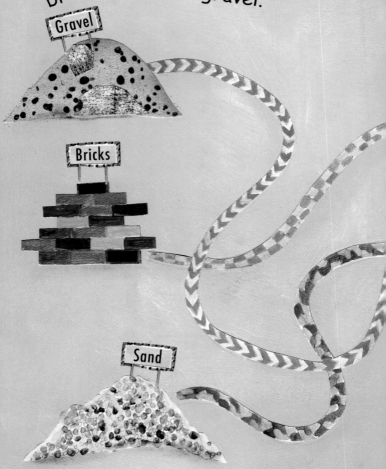

Can you follow their tyre tracks to find out which one brought which load?

These machines are building a road.
Can you spot the road roller?

Oh no! This digger has dug up a water pipe by mistake!

How many people are getting wet?

These drivers have forgotten where they parked their diggers.

Can you help to match them up?

Point to the bigger digger driver.
Point to the smaller digger driver.

Do you like to play with toy diggers?
Can you make a digger noise?

All the diggers have stopped work for the night.

Can you spot anyone who's not asleep?